Insights of a Psychoanalyst

Ruth Velikovsky Sharon, Ph.D.

Paradigma

Assisted by: Ryan Persichilli

Published by   Paradigma Ltd.
                    Internet: www.paradigma-publishing.com
                    e-mail: info@paradigma-publishing.com

ISBN 978-1-906833-04-6

Contents

Introduction

by Dylan Warner

My grandmother Ruth and her parents came to the United States from Palestine in 1939. My grandmother was born in Jerusalem in 1926. Her father Immanuel Velikovsky was born in Russia and her mother Elisheva Kramer was born in Germany. They met in Germany where Elisheva helped Immanuel write the plan to establish a Hebrew University in Jerusalem. Immanuel and Elisheva got married in 1922 in Germany and then moved to Palestine. Immanuel's parents moved from Russia to Palestine and Elisheva's father moved from Germany to Palestine.

In 1939 grandma Ruth's father, Immanuel, said that it was dangerous to live in what became Israel because World War II was about to happen. He also wanted to see the World's Fair in New York. He got tickets for himself, his wife, and two daughters (Ruth and Shulamit) to travel by boat to Italy. They boarded the boat in Haifa and the next day it stopped in Cyprus where Immanuel thought it was a mistake to travel to the US and they all got off the boat in Cyprus. After being in Cyprus for 3 hours he changed his mind again and got tickets to travel to Italy and then by train to France and then by boat to New York. When they got to New York they were not permitted to get off the boat because my great grandfather Immanuel brought too much money with him, they had Visitors Visas with them. As other passengers got off the boat, they remained on the deck and stared for hours at the sky scrapers. My grandmother Ruth feared that they were going to send them back to Israel, but instead they were transported to Elis Island and stayed there for hours until my great grandmother's brother, Siyfried Kramer, who lived in New York, got them released and took them by bus into Manhattan. They got off the bus on the corner of 72nd Street and Riverside Drive where my great grandfather rented a one room apartment.

Soon after they arrived in New York, Immanuel who knew Albert Einstein wanted to travel to Princeton and visit him. However, because of fear of traveling in Israel they were scared to travel from New York to Princeton. My great grandmother's niece had just gotten married and was killed by a bomb thrown into the kibbutz (a Jewish community) where she had gotten married. It was very dangerous to travel by bus from city to city in Israel because bombs were often thrown into the buses.

My grandmother Ruth never finished public school in Israel, and went on to high school in New York, where she was put in the second year. She used to speak Hebrew, everybody spoke English and some students were amazed.

One day, my great grandfather Immanuel began to go to Columbia University Library and the 42nd Street Library. He had an idea which he developed into a book. The name of the book was "Worlds in Collision". In 1950 the only book that outsold Immanuel's book was the Bible. The controversy about his book was very strong and while the book was #1 on the Best Seller list, the publisher, MacMillan gave it over to Doubleday. My grandmother remembers the excitement because scientists who didn't even read the book threatened not to buy any MacMillan books, if MacMillan continued to publish it. My great grandfather said repeatedly: "WHAT I AM AFRAID OF IS NOT TO BE DISPUTED, BUT TO BE DISMISSED WITHOUT BEING READ."

My great grandmother, Elisheva played the violin. In Germany she studied the violin with Adolf Busch and while in Israel she formed the Israel string quartet. She also said she was grateful she was born after Mozart.

Immanuel had gotten a medical degree in Russia and when he settled in Israel he decided to study psychology. He then travelled to Europe where he studied with Stekel, Jung and Freud. He saw Freud at the end of Freud's life. At that time Immanuel was the only psychoanalyst in Israel and worked from morning to night.

In 1950, my great grandmother Elisheva began studying sculpture at Columbia University with Maldarelli. One of her sculptures was chosen out of 5,000 submissions for a show at the Metropolitan Museum of Art, and it appeared on the first page of their catalogue.

After my grandmother Ruth graduated from High School, she went to New York University where she got her Bachelor's and Master's Degrees in art and then taught art for many years. One of her pupils was the daughter of the president of Princeton University. My grandmother's approach was to give students the material and a subject to paint. She never drew an example for them to copy and when they had exhibits all the children's pictures were included.

One time my great grandfather visited Albert Einstein and my grandmother Ruth went with him. She told me that Einstein was hunch backed, very pleasant as he took my grandmother to his yard to show her all the plants that were growing. His secretary was very helpful. My grandmother Ruth gifted my great grandfather's archives to Princeton University Library Special Collections. Included were letters from Freud and Einstein.

My grandmother Ruth earned a doctor's degree at the Union Graduate Institute and University. She received a PHD degree in Psychology. She also attended the Psychoanalytic Institute (CMPS) where she graduated and became one of the staff members. She still conducts group therapy on eight phones where the patients can hear each other.

Psychology

Psychoanalysis for Dummies

- In therapeutic situations, talking repairs damage. Psycho-analysis is all about words, not actions.

- What cures patients are the helpful responses from the analyst, not vindictiveness.

- Getting the patient to understand his or her problem does not resolve the problem or cure the patient during psycho-analysis.

- Getting rid of a feeling is impossible. During psychoanaly-sis, it's best to develop a new feeling to counteract the un-desirable feeling.

- A relationship between the patient and the analyst where the patient is able to say everything promotes the resolu-tion of problems.

- If the patient passes his therapist's advice to someone else, it could be as lethal as taking another person's medication; causing an "allergic" psychological reaction.

- Too often adults with the intention of being helpful give advice to their friends and family members that only a psy-choanalyst or medical doctor should divulge.

- A person who gives up the psychoanalytic treatment be-cause he had been advised by a friend or a new spouse on how to pursue his life, falls off the bridge which could have led him to success. He then drowns in a river of bad advice while everyone claims innocence.

● Some people live in a state of misery, not realizing that they are suffering from symptoms of a disorder that has remedies.

Psychoanalysts, Oh My!

● It is too tempting for a patient and/or analyst during the negative transference and counter transference period to act on their feelings and say, "goodbye."

● It is rare when both the patient and the analyst say "goodbye" at the same time, unless they are both vindictive.

● The analyst has to move slowly and carefully.

● The analyst must be careful not to fall into retribution and vindictive responses. If the patient disappears from treatment, the analyst cannot insist the patient return.

● If a patient's main problem is cutting off relationships with "goodbye," the patient becomes incurable because he will prematurely say goodbye to the analyst.

● If a patient says he is leaving treatment, the analyst should point to the fact that whatever he does in treatment he must also be doing elsewhere.

● If the analyst is vindictive, he may say, "Go!" and regret it later, but won't be able to reverse the impulsive goodbye.

● A patient is rarely afraid of the analyst saying, "Get out of here!"

- Most patients have one foot out the door throughout the analytic treatment.

- Patients often want to take control of the contract between them and the analyst.

- If analysts would not have to work so hard to keep patients from leaving, a lot more could be accomplished in the sessions in a shorter time, benefiting the patient.

- In the analytic relationship, the schedule of sessions and payments are all agreed upon and the resistances of the patient to obeying the contract are slowly resolved.

- In psychoanalysis, once transference develops, that person is "under the influence," feeling psychologically attached to the analyst.

- Too many analysts break up families, feeding into hatred between adult siblings and blocking conversations between old parents and their adult children.

- The analyst who advises a patient, "Stay away from your father, mother etc." steps out of his professional boundary.

- When a problem is resolved in treatment over a long period of time, another less toxic problem will appear.

- When a problem is overcome under pressure, a worse problem may replace it.

Fishing for the Problem

- What is so simple, obvious and helpful, yet has remained virtually unnoticed, is that whatever problems happen between the patient and the analyst in treatment are basically the patient's main problems in life.

- The analyst can say to the patient: "If I cure you of this problem right here between us, very gently and slowly, by working on it together, then you'll be able to cope in other situations like the one you are currently in with your family."

- When the patient takes control of the analytic contract and insists on making changes, such as how often he has sessions, how much he pays and when the payments are made, the patient is indirectly doing the analyst a favor by calling attention to the patient's main problem in life, which is taking control of relationships.

- The patient who goes from analyst to analyst because he doesn't want to pay is told: "This is your problem in other relationships as well. If you pay me the right amount at the end of each month, you will honor the contract and resolve your main problem."

- People wait and wait for the analyst to cure them. They don't realize that they must reach a point where they decide to change and change!

The Narcissist

- The narcissist is excessively sensitive, alternating between self-love and self-hate.

- Expecting his family to love him and orbit around his every whim, he is nevertheless very difficult to love. Living with a narcissist is a real challenge.

Suggestible People

- The negatively suggestible person will do the opposite of what is asked of him.

- People who are negatively suggestible to themselves will disregard their own decisions while overindulging their vices.

Depressed and Embarrassed

- In almost every family there is at least one person taking an antidepressant.

- People are often ashamed of having been prescribed antidepressants, being unaware of how prevalent it is.

Hopelessly Miserable

- A person who is continuously miserable induces in others the desire to get him out of their sight.

Analyzed vs. Unanalyzed

- The well-analyzed person speaks a "different language" than the unanalyzed.

- The analyzed is aware of his unconscious while the unanalyzed takes everything at face value.

- The well-analyzed person has the ability to say everything and hear everything.

Truth or Tall Tale

- In psychoanalytic treatment, when a patient tells the analyst that he (or she) was molested years ago, the psychoanalyst should listen in silence.

- Asking the patient questions about the reported molestation encourages the "memory," which is often exaggerated. One never knows if it really happened.

Monkey See, Monkey Induce

- People induce in others the predominant feeling their parents had for them.

- If one or both parents adored their child, the likelihood is that others will adore him throughout life.

- If a child was repeatedly spanked, he may induce in others the impulse to hit him or mistreat him in some way.

The Little Guy Hiding in Your Mind

- The unconscious mind knows "everything." Instinctive thoughts seemingly appearing from nowhere are the work of the unconscious mind.

We All Beg to Differ

- People experience contradictory feelings about every subject.

- If one takes a strong position supporting a feeling, it is more likely that whoever is listening will take the opposite position.

"You're Just Paranoid"

- The word "paranoid" could be a scapegoat for thieves, enabling them to steal.

- When a person repeatedly complains that he feels mistreated by someone, the one being accused must examine his words.

- Regardless if the accused person feels guiltless, he must be doing something to upset the complainer.

- To label the one feeling injured as "too sensitive," "imagining it" or "paranoid" s negligent.

- If something said is perceived by the listener as an attack, regardless of whether it was intended as an attack, it was an attack.

Fickle Like a Squirrel

- People who change their minds abruptly without warning could get "run over" like a squirrel that suddenly changes direction without notice.

- A person, whose feelings fluctuate rapidly back and forth like a strobe light, is emotionally unstable.

The Right Way to Question

- A question that includes the words, "How did that make you feel?" is an intrusive, ego-oriented question.

- An object-oriented question e.g. "where was that restaurant?" deals with facts and not feelings and thus keeps the person comfortable.

Art and Music

Life as a Cartoon

- The expression, "I see" often really means, "I understand." How did that become used so often? The reason is that we think by picturing things.

- We all think in pictures. Those who have the artistic ability can put them on canvas.

- The expression, "I can picture it", points to the visual images of the unconscious mind.

Conflicting Images with Reality

- When meeting someone face to face after having had an ongoing telephone conversation, it is difficult to abandon the initial imagined image. As a result, the two images fight for attention and take turns in one's mind.

Creativity of Mother Nature

- There are millions of people who, with the exception of identical twins, look different from one another.

- Were an artist to draw a million faces, no matter what, it would be very unlikely that they would all be different from one another. Nature is very creative and inventive.

Picasso Children

● Choosing the "best" picture among a child's drawings is subjective.

● Interpreting a child's art or asking a child to explain what he drew is intrusive. "I like your colors", "You will be an artist", and "This looks like your house" are intrusive comments.

● It is best to give a child paper, paints and a space to work. Telling a child what to draw and taking his pencil and drawing on his work is destructive.

● Paint-by-number and coloring books are, at best, uncreative. This includes crayons and coloring packets provided at restaurants.

Beethoven Children

● Parents don't realize that their children hear at a very young age, even within the womb, and it has an effect on them and how they react to it when they grow up.

● Hearing classical music in the home after birth allows the baby to experience music as a musical gift.

Daddy Needs a New Pair of Ear Lids

● Stores and restaurants that play jazz music over loud speakers make their patrons a "captive audience," whose only alternative is to depart, with fingers in both ears.

- When flipping through dozens of radio stations it is rare to hear music by Mozart, Haydn, Beethoven or other classical composers.

- A similar problem exists while on hold during a phone call, and one is "forced" to listen to music. We have no ear lids and often have no choice but to hang up since we can't plug our ears.

- Perhaps stores should provide customers with ear plugs or music that is played over a store's loudspeakers to be solely Mozart, Beethoven or Haydn. That may acquaint children with classical music.

Opera Singers

- Opera singers let out sounds through their mouths and then replenish the "loss" by putting food in their mouths, making them obese.

Sex

The Drive of Mankind

- The sexual drive keeps reproduction in our world.

"No! I Came From The Stork!"

- "My father, maybe. My mother, never!" The thought that one's parents engage in sexual intercourse paints a picture of what goes on behind closed doors.

- With few exceptions, all people on earth were conceived through sexual intercourse.

Mommy Loves Me More!

- The mother who frequently hugs, kisses and tickles her son, along with verbal praise, interferes with the son's relationship to his father and confuses the son's sexuality as he grows up.

- The mother, believing her son will love women because he has grown to love her so much, on the contrast, may breed a homosexual son.

- One mother used these words to confuse her son's sexuality, "You and I were lovers in a previous life."

- When a mother interferes with the father-son relationship, she undermines and unravels the son's identification with a male.

- A mother who showers in front of her son and gets dressed in front of her son unconsciously communicates that the son does not need another woman in his life.

- The son who recalls having seen his mother nude signals the break in the parent-child contract.

- The father usually does not realize the damaging effect this type of relationship between his wife and his son could be, so he fails to intervene.

- It is particularly important for a son to grow up identifying with his father.

Inter-Familial Rivalries

- When a father has a physically close relationship with his daughter, the daughter has difficulty indentifying with the mother.

- The mother will resent the daughter because she will feel that her husband loves the daughter more than he loves her, even if it isn't the daughter's fault.

- The daughter needs her mother's love and not being able to get it, the daughter may eventually seek a 'good breast' in another woman, which is a path towards lesbianism.

- On some unconscious level, a father may accept his daughter as a lesbian because he resents any man adoring the daughter who has become the 'love of his life'.

Touching Does Not Cure

- Mothers get more physical pleasure from contact with their sons than the sons do.

- Physical affection is stimulating to children. Such stimulation is not understood by children at a young age and they may long for more when they receive such stimulation.

- Shaking hands is an acceptable gesture for greetings and salutations.

- A child should not be asked to hug anyone. It is not an obligation to hug a member of the family.

- The parent who is accustomed to hugging will find it objectionable to give up or modify the touching habit.

- As soon as a child is able to sit by himself on a couch, the child does not require physical reassurance and assistance from a parent.

- Tickling and massaging children is too physically seductive and over gratifying.

In Worship

- It's common to see a mother or father sit at a religious service and physically attend to their children who are capable of attending as independent worshippers.

- Parents who try to communicate security and love to their children "force" other parishioners to observe their behavior.

- Any physical contact has some sexual overtones.

Perversion Excursions

- A sexual perversion is a serious psychological illness that is not easily cured.

- If someone reports ongoing contact with a sexual pervert, the listener should immediately inform a guardian (if the person has one) or law enforcement.

Baby

The Male Mentality

- An article in the New York Times on June 25th, 2007, reported that in the world one woman dies every minute of every day because of pregnancy and/or giving birth.

- Born male is a blessing because it is very physically and emotionally difficult to carry a baby to term and give birth.

- Fathers probably subconsciously celebrate when their wives give birth to boys, for those babies will never have to go through pregnancy and childbirth.

- Men have greatly underplayed that they walk from birth to death without ever having to go through pregnancy or child-birth.

- One father got it right when he sent his wife flowers on their child's birthday. He explained that she was the one who went through labor and child birth, so she deserved the flowers.

The Miracle of Birth

- To begin with, the miracle of creating a baby within one's body is beyond comprehension. When we eat, the food knows where to go, how to make blood, how to create urine and feces, and how to defecate to get rid of it. We take so much for granted.

- A father, on some unconscious level, must celebrate when his wife gives birth to a boy because he thinks, whether consciously or unconsciously, this is a lucky little baby. He's never going to have to go through pregnancy and child-birth as well as nursing.

- The physical enclosure of the womb provides nurturing and growth. Giving birth is the act of a fetus turning into an infant via the birth canal, thus entering the world.

- Birth was made clear. The baby enters the world from the mother's womb. That baby will die in a few minutes, hours or in a great many years. The baby does not have a date of death.

- When an amino reveals the sex of a fetus at sixteen weeks and the parents elect to wait and be "surprised" at the moment of birth, they don't fully accept the baby until birth. The surprise could be equally exciting at sixteen weeks.

Contracts

Breaking Contracts

- There are always "contracts" in every relationship, written, spoken and unspoken.

- Once a contract is broken by crossing a boundary, relationships become compromised and problems arise.

Parental Contracts

- Parents often are the worst culprits of breaking contracts by acting as friends towards their children.

- Parents will also break contracts with children being too affectionate psychologically and physically.

- When the parents break the contract with their children, the children will learn that it is okay to cross boundaries. This may create a liar that will lack remorse for it.

- When a father treats his daughter as though she is the love of his life, the daughter takes the love as a message that it is okay to cross boundaries and break contracts.

- The parent-child contract is: Parents provide a safe physical environment and oversee school work and musical practice.

- The parent-child contract IS NOT: "You are wonderful! You are terrific! You are adorable! You don't like green pants? Okay, let's find you another pair of pants that you'll like. Oh, you didn't do your homework? Let me help you with that sweetheart."

- An example of the parent-child contract IS: "You've had dinner, get into your pajamas. Brush your teeth, get to bed and goodnight. In the morning there will be breakfast, you'll get your books and we'll meet the bus."

- The bedtime parent-child contract should not be: "It's time for bed! Let me hug you and kiss you and wash you in the bathtub from head to toe and tuck you in." This is a prime example of a parent who breaks the parent/child contract.

- The contract between the father and the mother should be: When one parent says to the child, "Get to bed!" the other parent does not interfere in any way.

- Disciplining children with questions such as adding the word "OK?" confuses the contract.

- Parents have done a wonderful job if they brought up their children to remain on speaking terms with each other their entire lives. Sibling rivalry, which is normal, should not end their relationships.

Contractdiction

- There should never be contradiction in a contract, especially between parents and children.

- When the father tells the child to get to bed and the mother contradicts his discipline by silently showing disapproval with her posture and facial expressions, the mother jeopardizes the parental contract.

Miscellaneous Contracts

- Walking into a store, the shopper looks around and may ask for help and then goes to the register and pays, then receives a receipt and the purchased item is placed in a bag and the shopper leaves. This is an example of a contract.

- When a man goes into a store to buy something and flirts with the female cashier behind the counter, the contract is broken.

- In the analytic relationship, the schedule of sessions and payments are all agreed upon and the resistances of the patient to obeying the contract are slowly resolved.

Over Gratification

The Over Gratification Paradox

- Great damage is done to our world and to our future caused by the loving, kissy parent.

- Over Gratification is a paradox because parents feel that their children will benefit from the hugs, kisses, sweet words etc. However, the children will only be hindered.

- Announcing that the child is "astonishing", "unbelievable" and "incredible" leaves no room for modesty, sensibility and sanity.

- One of the worst mistakes is over-gratifying, over tending, over nurturing, buying too many gifts for the child, speaking only in soft tones and coddling the child who then becomes the focus of the house.

The Dangers of Over Indulgence

- Overindulging a child is tantamount to destroying his life.

- "You're beautiful, nothing can stop you now. You mean a lot to me, you're a good friend." Wait... Friend? Parents aren't supposed to be friends of their children!

- The disciplined child will identify with the positive qualities of each parent.

- On the other hand, the indulged child will identify with the negative qualities of each parent

- Parents set their children on a road to not accomplishing what the children should in studies, music and decency when they over gratify their children.

- Over-gratification creates emotionally and physically crippled adults whose success in life was snatched away.

- We must open our eyes and ears and look with a deep microscope into what's going on and prevent the next generation from bringing up their children in this similar way! "You're the best thing that ever happened. You're the sweetest and the loveliest and I adore you, you can't do anything wrong. I think you're the greatest. You are my friend. You deserve a big hug!" Then comes physical touching and kissing and Bravo!

Mr. Over-gratification

- The overindulged child grows up unequipped to take care of himself.

- The child, having been programmed by his parents to become a parasite, will look for a host to lean on.

- That child will occupy a throne from then on through old age, surrounding himself with people who take care of him.

- As a spouse, he demands to be treated as king and will select a spouse who will be a feather in his cap.

- If he cannot attain the success that he was told was "due" him, he will choose a partner who will put him "on the map."

- This person's career will be bogged down with hopes and schemes that go nowhere.

- If a child is treated as though he is fragile, he will become unaccustomed to hearing anything unpleasant and will talk incessantly.

- Children whose birthdays are celebrated ad nauseam will grow up expecting the spouse to carry on the tradition.

- Parents who tell their children, "All I want for you is to be happy in life," are giving them an impossible assignment, since happiness is elusive and, at best, intermittent. When their children grow up they will flounder from profession to profession looking for the profession that will make them happy. They will have difficulty settling down with one partner as they search for happiness. It's an unachievable assignment and, ironically, a life sentence of unhappiness.

Notorious C.I.G. (Children Indulged & Gratified)

- The overindulged child will become obsessed with wanting to have his name in lights, having been repeatedly told "you are special!"

- To keep from being a loser, the overindulged child will attempt to make others feel jealous of him.

- The over gratified child will focus on marrying a celebrity, owning designer clothes and owning a big house.

Hallowed Be My Child's Name

- Some parents think that places of worship are where they should show love, affection and security to their children.

34

- They are physically attentive to their children, even when the children are perfectly capable of sitting up as independent worshipers.

"Good Job, Bobby!"

- Convinced that to overlook their child's every little accomplishment is neglect, parents don't realize that the child will attain more if his minor accomplishments are not applauded.

- Parents who demand that their children do their homework and practice their musical instruments daily, are caring parents.

- Parents who tell their children, "All I want is for you to be happy in life" are giving them an unachievable assignment.

- Happiness is elusive and at best, intermittent.

Breeding Liars, Thieves and Criminals

- When a parent manipulates a game he plays with his child so the child wins, he teaches the child dishonesty

- The overindulged child will grow up spreading unfounded accusations about others.

- The consequence of overindulgence is the creation of a liar, who lacks remorse.

- The behavior of a dishonest child propels into adulthood, endangering the marital partner.

- Parents continue to defend and compliment their grown overindulged offspring, who has become deceptive.

- When an overindulged child does something deceptive, people have a hard time believing it because the child is so sweet and knows how to act innocent.

Womb Service

- A child who is raised by overindulgent parents never ventures out of the "womb," yet parents rarely heed the warning.

- A good rule for parents to abide by is: Don't do for the child what he can do for himself.

- An overindulged child will at every stage of development, employ the words "I can't" or "Help me."

- Making a child do things on his own sets the direction for eventual independence, although acquired slowly.

- This is far less painful for parents and children than independence gained in a harsh way during the teen years.

Not In My House!

- A house that is a dictatorship where the parents are the boss and the child obeys, where the deadly "disease" of over-gratification does not flourish, breeds successful adults.

- The parent who is a disciplinarian, laying down limits and boundaries, will bring up a child who will know limits and boundaries, not "whatever I want, is mine!"

- When the father says, "Get to bed" and the mother silently, with her posture and facial expression, communicates she disapproves, the mother jeopardizes the discipline.

- Particularly lethal is the over-gratifier of the two parents who supervises and insists that the other parent conform to the over-gratifying approach.

- Parents who contradict each other: "He's tired. He's hungry. Let him rest a little. Let him have some fun" are damaging their children as well as their marriage.

- Parents who use questions to rebuke their children, such as "When are you going to stop fighting?" or "Why haven't you cleaned your room?" are not really soliciting answers.

- When a parent, as a disciplinary act, tells his child to go to his room for an assigned period of time, saying, "When you stop crying you can come out", puts the child in control, diminishing the discipline.

- Parents should provide a safe physical and emotional environment and oversee their offspring's homework and music schedules. The offspring should obey.

- If the stricter parent succumbs to the overindulgent parent, the child, through no fault of his own, is sent down the path of failure.

- The parent who tries to supervise the other parent in the presence of the child, ("You are too mean to Robbie. All he said was 'I won't do it'. What is so terrible if Robbie says 'no' to you?") undoes the discipline and neither parent carries authority.

Generation Over-gratification

● Parents who themselves were overindulged will perpetuate the problem and raise overindulged children, the problem continuing from generation to generation.

● A new psychological formula must be encompassed in order to understand how a father who worships his daughter, and a mother who worships her son, ruin the child's lives.

A Boomerang Named Indulgence

● The country has to learn that as much as the intention of raising adored, worshipped children sounds good – it boomerangs!

● The over gratified child will ultimately contribute mayhem to our society.

● Parents who overindulge their child from the very beginning of life never raising their voice, while giving the child whatever he wants, ruin the child's life.

● When once a year a parent raises his voice, commanding the child do his homework or clean the room, the parent sets on an alarm.

● Being unaccustomed to discipline the child will recall these occurrences as ongoing monumental abuse throughout his childhood.

● Helping children in many ways, then when they still need help, the parent who deploys one rigid "no more" puts the children on to the road of failure.

The Degrees of Overindulged Children

- When the parents stopped the over-gratifying approach will reflect directly on how the damage from over-gratification may be reversed.

- The tragedy of a child being over gratified is that as an adult it is almost impossible, or at least extremely difficult, to reverse the damage.

- Unfortunately, overindulgent parents meaning well, offer sweet words to their children as they grow up, until it's too late to reverse the damage.

- If the child was two when the over-gratification stopped, the chances of the damage being reversed are good.

- If the child is five and already has trouble at school and on the playground, it will be difficult, but not impossible to reverse.

(Don't) "Get Physical, Physical!"

- Physical affection, as reassuring as it may appear to the parents, may actually be experienced by the child as too seductive and too possessive.

- For a parent to sit on the couch and watch TV with a child and have an arm around the child, regardless of age, is a mistake.

- As soon as a child is able to sit up by himself on the couch, he doesn't need physical reassurance that the parents love him.

- Tickling children on the back or arm is too seductive.

Diabetes of the Mind

- After a 13 year old gave his Bar Mitzvah speech, his mother stood up and expressed her feelings about what he had said. Some of the adjectives the mother used: "sensational, terrific, astounding, inspirational, enormous, outrageous, unbelievable, incredible, impressive beyond belief."
  The son developed "diabetes of the mind," an emotionally overwhelming reaction to sweet words.
  Meaning well, the mother nevertheless put him in a world where reality did not exist.
  As a result, the son required discipline to put him back into the real world.
  Reminded that he had gotten a lot of help, he acknowledged and thanked all the people who helped him and then concentrated on his studies.

- Too much sweetness bestowed upon a child, even a 13 year old, creates an emotional imbalance that is difficult to cure.

- There is no antidote, no insulin to counteract the sweet serum of words the he absorbed that triggered the emotional diabetes.

Smile like You Mean It

- A smile is worth words. Parents should replace physical affection with smiling.

- Don't treat the child as if the child came down from heaven and is the greatest thing ever.

- It is true that it's a miracle that we can create babies, but we have got to drop the notion that we've got to make our children feel special!

Cookie Monsters

- The overeater does not savor what is in his mouth unless it is accompanied by seeing there is more on his plate ready for the next mouthful!

- One should appreciate the three T's of food: Taste, Texture, and Temperature.

An Overdone Christmas and a Wasteful New Year

- As a collective result of over gratification in our society, each calendar holiday begins with intense pre-holiday preparation and ends with post-holiday recuperation, so the country is repeatedly "shut down" for three days or more, where work, school and government come to a halt.

Parents of the Opposite Sex

- When the relationship between mother and son, or the relationship between father and daughter go out of the boundary of parent/child contract, damage can be severe.

- This relationship may affect the child's sexuality. It may send the child down a road of disappointment and despair.

- The father who indulges his son does not confuse the boy's sexuality, although overindulging a child is destructive

- Similarly, the mother who overindulges her daughter makes her spoiled, lazy, dishonest and unsuccessful. However, lesbian feelings won't be induced as a result.

- While both parents may act overly kindly, there are different effects relative to the gender of the parents and the children.

- Crossing boundaries as parents, becoming the childrens' 'lovers', confuses the childrens' roles throughout life.

- Announcing that their child is 'astonishing' and 'incredible' leaves no room for modesty, sensibility or sanity.

- A teenage boy dancing with his mother at a social occasion, or a father dancing with his teenage daughter, contrary to what the parents may think, is destructive.

- Children should not be instructed to make physical contact with a parent, grandparent or anyone else.

- A hug goodnight and a hug in the morning before the child departs for school are acceptable boundaries.

- Parents get more pleasure from the closeness to their children than the children do.

- Parents need to limit their praise and affection to avoid hurting their children in the long run.

- People induce in other people the main feeling their parents had for them. If a person was brought up in harsh way with a lot of spanking, then, as he grows up, that person will induce in others the feeling of wanting to spank him. If the person was adored growing up, being a Daddy's Girl or Mommy's Boy, people will adore them.

Pinocchio Syndrome

- A person who lies once is no longer trustworthy.

- There is only one truth. Getting in trouble for telling the truth is a compliment.

- White lies are still lies. Telling a lie creates a stream of lies, each covering a previous lie.

- The person who lies often will believe his own lies.

Truth Is...

- The person who says, "The truth is," should be asked, "Was the rest a lie?"

- There is only one truth and once these words sink in, it is very easy for one to only tell the truth.

Generational Dishonesty

- Parents are responsible for bringing up an offspring who is deceptive and dishonest

- We must open our eyes and ears and observe closely what is going on so we can prevent the next generation from being brought up with exaggerated praise.

- Parents who are consistently truthful with their children as well as with others will raise honest children.

- It is far better for a child to deal with all feelings mobilized by every situation than to "spare" the child, thereby sending him onto a path of not believing his parent and not holding the truth in high esteem.

- If a child hears a parent lying to someone else, that will have a negative impact on the child, no matter how truthful the parent is with the child.

- As the saying goes, the apple doesn't fall far from the tree. Children grow up with similar qualities to the parent, including dishonesty.

- Children who are brought up with lies and misrepresentations will get in trouble with the law when older.

- The parent who, when playing with a child, manipulates the game so the child wins every time, teaches the child not to tolerate the frustration of losing, as well as dishonesty. The child will be unprepared to live in the real world.

- How does the legend of Santa Claus play itself out as a child gets older and discovers that it was, in essence, a fairy tale? This is a national symbol and is a cultural lie that few parents tamper with.

Too Much Information (TMI!)

- It may be destructive to give children information they did not request.

- It's not the parents' job to come home and say to their child, "My boss yelled at me today and I think I'm going to be fired."

- It's not as if the child asked, "Why are you so crabby, daddy?" There is a difference between volunteering the truth and responding truthfully to a child's inquiries.

- There are exceptions, such as a parent coming back from a parent-teacher conference hearing a request from the teacher to inform the child that he has been too unruly in class.

- In this situation, the parent does not have to wait for the child to inquire about the conference; neither should the parent ask the child if he wants to know what the teacher said.

- It is very destructive to tell a child, or even a grownup, that his parents did not love him.

- In the case of a divorce, one parent badmouthing the other parent around the child only hurts the child.

- Similarly, not telling the child the truth about who his real daddy is will harm the child

- The truth once discovered, will cause trauma for the child who has learned that the parent he always thought was his biological parent was in fact not.

Not Available, Please Leave a Message

- When a secretary's response to a caller who asks to speak to the boss is, "He is away from his desk," or "He is on a conference call," when in fact, the boss is signaling, "I'm not here!" symbolizes a schism in the trust between the secretary and the boss.

Thievery

- Some animals steal the eggs of other species.

- Thievery in the human race is prevalent, where partners, ideas and possessions are stolen.

- The thief steals material possessions as well as the victim's good reputation. Should the thief be accused, he will be outraged and will cut off contact with the victim.

- When a person is careless about his possessions and the possessions include precious items, it tempts the dishonest person to steal and to be sneaky in personal relationships.

- Once a victim becomes aware of what had happened, the thief creatively and maliciously adds insult to the injury, calling the victim paranoid.

- When a teenager commits a crime such as a theft, his parents should go to court! That is the only solution for people to become aware of this huge problem of sweet, loving, overindulged people telling lies.

- The "professional" thief ignores the bill collector and disregards delinquency notices for as long as the thief can get away with it.

- The thief knows how to manipulate the legal system, and to be sneaky in personal relationships.

- People cannot adjust to the fact that Daddy's Girls or Mommy's Boys do not tell the truth! If one looks at it closely, one discovers that that is, in fact, true!

Empathy

- A person who callously commits a crime, ignoring the victim's fear and pain, and only betrays panic and fear when he himself is on the witness stand, lacks empathy.

- Early in life the quality of empathy develops, but for some people it never develops at all, especially in the case of Daddy's Girls and Mommy's Boys, who essentially are narcissists. They only have empathy for themselves.

Kyle A. Knuppel, a medical student, wrote the lyrics for this song, *The Stranger's Land*, which shows his deep empathy for Sgt. Jeremy Feldbusch, a soldier who was blinded in Iraq

> You can never understand
> The anger I have within.
> The last thing I'll ever see
> Is my life flashed before me.
>
> I say to myself everyday
> "Others have it worse"
> But the pain just grows and grows
> All I feel is hurt
>
> I've been called a hero
> Like others who have gone before
> What's more is that I understand
> The hell that they call war.

After they write my story down
Over and over
I'll take what I hold dear
And hold it even closer

I'm home now
I can feel love all around
I know somehow,
I'll come around

In my mind's eye
Things have changed forever.
I'm alive
I need to feel it more
Than ever

Daddy's Girl

The 'Angel' on the Pedestal

- The father who adores his daughter from day one, compounding it by talking to her only in the most loving ways, sets the daughter on a road of lifetime disappointments.

- Daddy wanted his little girl to be happy, happy, happy! He adored her to an immeasurable degree.

- He said things like, "You are adorable, beautiful and wonderful. Everything you do is great."

- He will put her on a pedestal, and at times will ignore his wife in order to attend to his daughter

- The father will lavish affection with toys, vacations and attention, using sweet words and phrases towards his daughter to make her feel special.

- The father means well, thinking that his daughter will grow up having an example of a loving male and will search for the perfect husband to attend to her 'perfect' self.

- The daughter unfortunately will become spoiled and lazy, rarely achieving her goals in life.

Looking for the 'Good Breast'

- As a result of a close father/daughter relationship, the daughter will often have a hostile relationship with her mother.

- The mother will grow jealous of her daughter because the father adores the daughter so much.

- Daughters need their mothers' love, yet they won't get it if the father treats the daughter as the 'love of his life'.

- This may lead to lesbianism since the daughter was resented by her mother. She will then look for the 'good breast' in other women.

- The father's love of the mother is displaced by his love for the daughter, who has become addicted to admiration and attention.

Here Comes the Bride, Her Mouth Fat with Lies

- As a result of being adored incessantly, Daddy's girls, as well as Mommy's boys, become secretive and deceptive.

- People have difficulty understanding that a Daddy's girl and Mommy's boy will never be forthright.

- When the father treats his daughter as though she is "the love of his life", the daughter will learn that crossing boundaries is acceptable.

- This will lead her to cross other boundaries, becoming a liar and a manipulator.

- Consequentially, her father will become a lifelong 'slave' to Daddy's girl.

- When she says, "I'm going to make this work", she knows she won't.

- Day and night, words that come out of her mouth are rarely honest.

- Daddy's girls grow up convinced they never do wrong and always deserve praise and applause.

- Daddy's girls in psychoanalytic treatment still are incurable. Their brain dictates dishonesty. If there is a Daddy's girl in your life you better guard your wallet.

Mr. Right and Mrs. Wrong

- Being adored by her father, the daughter will enter into an unfulfilling marriage or will remain single, never finding the "right man."

- She will have had examples of an adoring and loving male and will know what she wants in a husband.

- She will have a "daddy" script and symbolic cue cards for her husband to recite.

- She will direct him by choosing words and tones that she wants him to say to her.

- If the husband doesn't comply with her desires, she will admonish him, "You didn't even kiss me good morning" and "Aren't you proud of me for the meal I prepared?"

- No matter who a Daddy's girl marries, the husband will not be able to fulfill his wife's expectations.

- She will likely marry a successful, intelligent man, who will not recognize that his wife is a Daddy's girl, dishonest and deceptive as a result of her upbringing.

- Since her husband will not fulfill her Daddy's girl's expectations, she may seek love elsewhere, becoming promiscuous with other men.

- One married Daddy's girl had an affair with another man. She thought she deserved compliments and incessant love.

- If a husband does not compliment his wife ad nauseum like her father did, she sulks and badmouths him.

- Nevertheless, the husband will remain an enabler, believing his wife is honest.

- She will go around badmouthing her husband, faking innocence, diminishing her husband's reputation.

- The husband will not believe she is dishonest because she was taught how to play the 'I didn't do it" game.

- When told that his wife had badmouthed him or cheated on him, the husband will not believe it.

- She will interfere with her husband's disciplining their children, "They're tired. They're hungry."

- She'll supervise him, saying things like "Leave them alone", causing him to over-gratify their children.

- A woman who says, "My father is (was) my best friend," her potential husband better reconsider.

- The husband may later say, "When we got married, I had no idea she'd be like this."

- Nevertheless, the clues were there, but were either disregarded or expected to disappear. In reality the problems became exacerbated.

- If the Daddy's girl and her husband get divorced, the Daddy's girl will come off sweet and the decent husband will not reveal his wife's duplicitous nature.

Mommy's Boy

The "Mommy Stimulus" Plan

- When a mother adores her son with hugs, kisses and touching, she is ultimately ruining the boy's life.

- Where did the mother get the idea that her son needs a lot of physical contact and that the child will feel neglected and unloved if the mother does not give him physical attention?

- Mothers who watch TV with their sons and have an arm around their shoulders are too intimate.

- A lot of physical affection over-stimulates the son, creating physical sensations in him that the son doesn't understand at a young age.

It's Not in the Genes! It's the Means!

- The extent of his mother showing affection towards her son can influence his sexuality.

- A mother should not behave like her son's 'lover' or friend. When this boundary is crossed, there will be serious consequences.

- When the mother says things like, "Oh you look so good, you're so adorable! Let me kiss your cheek ten times! Come here and give me hugs and kisses. Let me sing to you and hold you," she damages her son.

- Mothers have to abide by the parent-child contract and not cross boundaries, or the damage will be severe.

- The mother who says to her son, "You are the greatest! You are handsome!" thinks that he will grow up adoring women.

- When grown up, women won't interest him. No woman will ever appear as psychologically or physically interesting to him as his mother.

- When a mother is seen by her son in a state of undress, this unconsciously communicates to the son that he does not need another woman in his life.

- Homosexuality is not in the genes. It is in his upbringing.

Father-Son Ties

- When a son has a good relationship with his father, he will identify with his father and grow up heterosexual.

- If the father does not give any input into the son's life, the child will suffer.

- The father rarely realizes that the relationship between the mother and son is damaging the son. He therefore fails to intervene.

- If the father is in the picture at all, he will resent the son for taking over his wife and will look askance at their relationship.

- If the father is a disciplinarian, the son may escape the problem.

- If the mother interferes with the son's identification with his father, she undermines and unravels the son's hetero-sexuality.

Mommy's Little Liar

- People have great difficulty in adjusting to the fact that Mommy's boys, just like Daddy's girls, are not forthright and look to deceive.

- Yet despite their sneaky behavior, everyone trusts them. When they do something sneaky, everyone becomes momentarily disturbed, while still adoring.

- Being fantastic actors, Mommy's boys and Daddy's girls make the person who accuses them of being dishonest or stealing look stupid.

Lying: A Circle of Hell

- If a person was adored growing up, chances are high that the person will be adored throughout life. People induce in others the predominant feeling their parents had for them.

- Daddy's girl or Mommy's boy steal and get away with it.

- When caught, people momentarily don't trust them, yet they are still adored.

- When Mommy's boy and Daddy's girl get in trouble for stealing, they don't know how to get out of the mess.

- They often choose a path of 'getting out', which digs them into deeper trouble.

- They will take something that doesn't belong to them, hide it, and then hide that they hid it.

- Instead of confessing and apologizing, they take things because they believe they deserve whatever they want.

- When told, "Just confess you did it and let bygones be bygones", Daddy's girl and Mommy's Boy panic, covering their tracks over and over, while emotionally spiraling downhill.

- The fact that they could be "found out" occupies their mind.

- Their children might begin to suspect that their mother and father are lying. This will affect their school work as well as their ability to function.

- In divorces, Daddy's girl and Mommy's boy manipulate the outside world, making it seem like it was the decent partner's fault that the divorce happened.

- The outside world falls for the act, blaming the decent partner for the divorce and leaving the Daddy's girl or Mommy's boy seemingly innocent.

- The best solution is for people to become aware of this problem that encompasses us: Overindulged children grow up often telling lies.

Depression and Anger

Suppressed Anger Breeds Depression

- There is little as physically and emotionally debilitating as depression, which is anger turned inward, depleting the mind of hope.

Anger Outlets

- Saying once to the person causing the anger, "I'm angry at you", is "medicine" which can relieve the reactive depression (a depression caused by a reaction to an ongoing situation).

- Rage does not evaporate. A person must recognize the existence of rage within him, and then must verbalize it in small measures.

- Uncontrollable, ongoing expressed anger is a symptom of emotional illness.

- Screaming, yelling and punching as a therapeutic outlet is ineffective. Mental hospitals are full of people who cannot control their rage.

- A person's anger "department" is never empty. Telling someone to freely express his anger is destructive, for no matter how many angry words are unleashed there will always be more pent-up rage.

- Anger has channels by which it travels without harming its owner or recipient.

- Anger expressed in "dirty" looks, silence or staying away accomplishes nothing.

- Biting one's fingernails prevents one from scratching the "enemy". In the same way, letting one's teeth rot prevents putting into action the temptation to bite the "enemy". Both are measures of controlling aggression.

- Although tears are associated with sorrow and pain, tears may also be an expression of anger.

- In the case of losing someone, there may be a component of anger at having suffered a loss.

Anger Volcano

- The very quiet person, not speaking on any issue, often hoards a volcano of rage for a periodic release at home. Appearing complacent to the outside world, he often counts on his family not to betray his dual personality.

- People either suffer in silence or complain incessantly attempting to draw others into their state of mind.

Regret Breeds More Regret

- Regret ruins the present as the past was "ruined" and as one man summed it up "I regret that I regret".

- Instead of bemoaning their fate and indulging in regret, people who walk "between the raindrops" looking for rainbows avoid major emotional "storms".

- In almost every family there is at least one person on anti-depressants. People are ashamed of having been prescribed antidepressants, being unaware of how prevalent it is.

Resilience Shows Character

- A person's emotional health is measured by his degree of resilience. If he recovers from a narcissistic, emotional injury in ten minutes, he is emotionally healthy. If it takes him two hours, it is a borderline case. If it takes him four hours or more, or if he brings up the problem again and again, he is emotionally unstable.

- A person who gives either a warm greeting or a snub-one never knows what to expect-may seem innocent, but, in fact, is actively hostile and manipulative.

Goodbye

A Self-Burial in a Lonely Graveyard

- Too often people kill relationships abruptly and permanently, not allowing the other person involved to come up with a solution other than killing off the relationship.

- Decapitating a person with a final sentence "I want you out of my life" is an act of vindictiveness.

- The shunned person should recognize that the rejecting person has proven that he is not forthright.

- Someone who rejects others is buried permanently in a psychological cemetery

The Silent War

- Silence can be used as a hostile weapon in a "vindictive war".

- When people's phone calls are never answered and e-mails are ignored, they will find themselves at a 'castle wall', where the castle is named 'Vindictive'.

- On the other hand, the person who returns every phone call has the self-esteem and the ability to politely end undesirable conversations. This person deserves the Purple Heart for his courage.

- Ignoring someone by not greeting him is an effective way of symbolically slaying the person.

- When people express their rage with silence, they are planting a proverbial 'bomb'. The victims of silence don't know how to defuse the 'silent bomb' and therefore are forced to run away, leaving the problem unresolved.

- A person who slams down a phone or storms out of a room communicates the threat of an 'attack' of vindictive silence.

- The vindictive person is capable of making a momentary reaction permanent.

- People who talk things out instead of acting out avoid ambushes, which forces attackers to return.

Judge a Book by Its Integrity

- When finding fault with someone, one should look at the person's core, his essence. Is the person honest? Loyal?

- Criticizing a person for being sloppy, moody, or not affectionate should fade away in the big picture.

The Fool and the Wise Man

- The person who postpones an impending agreement in the hope of winning an advantage may discover that the other person will use the time to reconsider his own position.

- While the fool thinks it over, the wise man does too!

- A man asked a woman he was dating to marry him. She said "No," but a few weeks later she reconsidered. He turned her down, stating that if she had really wanted to marry him she would have said "yes," when he had asked for her hand in marriage the first time.

And the Academy Award Goes To...

- Too often Daddy's girls and Mommy's boys are the ones who say "I want you out of my life!" because the parent of the opposite sex set the example of crossing boundaries.

- Daddy's girls and Mommy's boys are deceptive actors often deserving the Academy Award! Their spouse, if they have one, is usually bright yet naïve and will fall for the act while his reputation is ruined.

The Mediocre Joker

- The jealous mediocre who has a position of power too often slams the door on the talented. As a result, mediocrity reigns.

Psychoanalysts' Troubles

- In psychoanalytic treatment, if a patient's main problem is breaking off relationships and fighting a 'silent war' through vindictiveness, the patient becomes incurable.

- The patient is incurable because if told of his problem, he may disappear from treatment. The psychoanalyst can insist "Stay!" but it won't work.

- This "goodbye" resistance discourages the psychoanalyst from being forthright. How can the analyst resolve a problem if the patient goes out of the picture?

Just Do It

- Once reading this chapter, a person who has decided to end a relationship abruptly should reconsider and reconnect with the shunned person. We are not animals. We have words!

Death

Life is a Death Sentence

- Life is a death sentence, that's for sure, only we don't know when or how or where we will die. Once we are born, we are ultimately going to die.

- The only tolerable part of death is that once dead, the person doesn't know he is dead.

- Some religions will disagree.

From Alpha to Omega

- Birth was made very clear. The baby enters the world from the mother's womb. That baby will die in a few minutes, hours or years. It does not have a date of death.

- Once born, and beginning to understand the subject of life and death, the everlasting fear of death begins to grow until it becomes a subject which prevails our lives.

- Being offered such a fascinating life, the awareness of eventual death becomes more and more overwhelming.

Religion as a Death Buffer

- Religion diminished the fear of dying by creating afterlife. Because religion becomes a major source of "comfort" and a solution to the hovering death fright, it is seen as kind.

- There is panic, fear and anxiety at the thought of life ending.

Effect of Death on Psych

- We experience the future in our thoughts while we are still alive, so we, in a sense, will be there.

- When attending a memorial service it is important to communicate to the survivor how helpful he or she had been to the deceased. The close survivors, with few exceptions, experience guilt, regardless of whether the guilt is based on fact.

- Too often adult children remember their childhood as "abusive" and proceed to retaliate against their aged parents by neglecting or criticizing them when the parents are near the end of life. All parents make mistakes. However, they helped give the greatest gift of all, life.

The Hypochondriac's Burden

- The hypochondriac believes that he faces imminent death every day of his life, an all encompassing, and burdensome, emotional illness.

- The hypochondriac never asks that last question of his doctor in order to be fully assured, knowing full well that there will still be another question, and the reassurance will only last moments. Hypochondriacs die too so their complaints cannot be disregarded.

Suicidal or Sympathetic, That is the Question

- A person who says "I'm suicidal" could be saying it as blackmail in order to give him what he wants, such as cigarettes. It's risky not to believe that person and it's risky to believe the person.

- Those who commit suicide lack sympathy for family members and peers who care for them. Suicide affects more than just the victim; it affects society, and it affects society negatively.

Insured Death: Life Insurance Scams

- A life insurance policy selected a date of death for the insured where the coverage no longer exists. Knowing this causes the insured to hope to die before that date. It is a death sentence.

The Importance of a Living Will

- Children whose parents do not have a living will may make a life or death decision for their parents, which potentially could leave a scar of guilt.

- Parents control their children's lives and destiny by assigning two siblings, who don't get along, as executors of their will.

- Not having a written will or leaving more to one child will cause acrimony, dissent and misery after the parent's death. The inheritance will be spent on lawyers.

Trained to Kill

- There was a recent New York Times front page story about veterans becoming killers. Parents whose offspring kill are considered legally innocent. Surely these parents did something wrong in bringing up a killer. The owners of a dog that killed a neighbor some years ago received a severe jail sentence, although recently amended.

- Should the heads of government be held legally accountable for an army veteran who has been taught to kill, commit murder once discharged? The dog may have been taught to kill, but so was the draftee.

- One tolerable part of death is that once dead the person doesn't know he is dead.

- Another tolerable part about death is that if one has created something during a lifetime, it endures through many generations.

- A suicidal person wants to kill someone else and instead kills himself. In the case of a suicide bomber, he kills himself and kills others at the same time, but makes it appear a selfless act.

- Life is a temporary condition. When one dies, the world will disappear.

- One's essence, unique as a fingerprint, begins early in life and is intent on keeping the person alive. It is the person's psychological DNA which shows up in the person's every activity as well as in dreams.

- Once born and beginning to understand the subject of life and death, the everlasting fear of death begins to grow and grow, until it becomes a subject which prevails in our life.

Words

"Animals bite, growl and fight,
People have language.
We are not animals,
We have words."

The Art of Conversation

- A comment can have different meanings depending on the pitch, intensity, intonation and volume of a person's voice, as well as the speed of his words.

- Correctly anticipating the listener's reaction to one's words before the words are uttered shows good judgment. If, on the other hand, the listener's reaction is unexpected, such as a verbal explosion or total silence, the talker's judgment was incorrect. It is best to review the situation and the next time, reconsider the approach.

- It is important to anticipate a listener's reaction to one's words before the words are said. If the reaction is unexpected the talker's judgment was off, unless that reaction was desired.

- Saying once to the person causing the anger: "I am angry at you" is "medicine" which could relieve the reactive depression.

- Before taking a tough, uncompromising position, a person has to be realistic about what rung on the ladder he is on. If a person misjudges his position, he may be setting himself for a tumble.

- Some people make others feel good with every communication, while other people make people feel bad with almost every communication. Neither is genuine nor productive.

- Persuasion is a form of torture for both the persuader and the one being persuaded. It is hard work to try to convince a skeptic. On the other hand, resisting an onslaught of unsolicited, persuasive arguments is exhausting. Regardless of who wins, the relationship is strained.

- The person who says one thing, and does another makes his words meaningless.

What People Really Mean

- The person who gives either a warm greeting or a snub, may seem innocent, but in fact is hostile and manipulative.

- The words "deserve" and "entitled" belong in a legal or religious dictionary.

- If the answer to the question "Am I upsetting you?" is "no", it is an unconscious invitation to try harder to upset the person. If the answer is "yes", the mission had been "accomplished".

- Anyone who says "Trust Me" is presumptuous.

- Saying "no problem" when having been confronted by a big problem is a lie.

- The unreturned phone call, unanswered letter and snubbing someone keeps the issue between them unresolved.

Debate vs. Attack

- People experience contradictory feelings about every subject. If one takes a strong position supporting one feeling, it is likely that the listener will take the opposite position.

- Making a request of someone can be imposing. It is best to wait for an invitation.

- A question that includes the words, "How did that make you feel?" is an intrusive, ego-orientated question. An object-orientated question like "Where was the restaurant?" deals with facts and not with feelings, and therefore, does not attack the ego, keeping the person comfortable.

- When a person repeatedly complains to someone that he feels mistreated by him, the one being accused must examine his actions. Even if the accused feels guiltless, he or she must be doing something to upset the complaining person.

- To label one who feels injured from an attack as "too sensitive", "imagining it" or "paranoid" is negligent.

Gooey Gossip

- Anyone can say anything derogatory about anyone and regardless if it is partially true or not true at all, some of it "sticks". One's reputation travels with one forever. A person can be harmed by untruths spread about him.

- Those that gossip want themselves to seem good while making the one being talked about to seem evil, when in fact, it's the opposite.

- "It's none of my business" is a set of brakes not often applied by the one who does not wish to be a listener to gossip. Not stopping the gossiper provides the listener with intimate details about another, which if true, he would have rather not known, and which he can never forget nor verify.

Mindless Conversation

- Taken literally, a response to the frequently inserted "you know" between sentences should be "Why are you telling me if I know?" The response to the frequent space filler, "I don't know" should be "Then why do you keep talking about it if you don't know?" "You know what I mean" should be responded to with "What do you mean?" How could anyone know what a person means?

- If a person's greeting is, "Hello, How are you?" the answer is, regardless of the truth, "Good". As the person departs he is instructed "Have a good one" or "have a wonderful day" or "enjoy!"

Diarrhea of the Mouth

- The unconscious purpose of compulsive talking is to prevent the listener from jumping in and possibly saying something hurtful.

- From day one of his life, if a child is treated as though he is fragile and is talked to only in loving tones while keeping all noise away, he will be unaccustomed to hearing anything unpleasant. He will talk incessantly, filling spaces between sentences with "I mean" or "you know what I mean?" He will also give redundant details when describing a situation, so the listener will not be able to participate in the conversation.

- A caller who leaves a lengthy phone message, and at the end quickly rattles off his phone number, forces the listener to listen to the entire message again and again in order to get the correct number.

- Lengthy phone greetings are tedious. E.g. "Hello, you have reached the Smiths: David, Ellen, Jeremy, Rebecca and Betty. None of us are at home, but if you leave a message of any length, we will be sure to call you back. Thank you very much for calling and have a great day. Goodbye." In contrast, "You have reached the Smiths, Please leave a message", is respectful of the caller's time.

Breaking a Broken Record

- The more you explain the less they understand. Many details provide the listener with reasons to disagree, argue, or simply misunderstand. It is tiresome to listen to "endless words".

- When a problem is brought up again and again and the arguments go in "circles", chances are that one of the participants is emotionally unstable. Under such circumstances, it is advisable to terminate the conversation and pursue a solution at a later date, under different circumstances.

- Those who are trying to get their way don't want to compromise. They incessantly argue, until the other person agrees to the demands.

Silence Isn't Always Golden

- Animals bite, growl and fight. People have language; we are not animals, we have words!

- Silence can be used as a hostile tool. Deprived of "clearing the air", unable to communicate with one who expresses rage with silence, there is no alternative but to eventually become silent oneself, leaving the misunderstanding unresolved.

- The unreturned phone calls, the unanswered letters, snubbing someone, are all ways people act out hostile feelings leaving a problem unresolved.

Word Discipline

- Growing up, if a child is permitted to disregard the parents' commands, he will eventually write his own dictionary where "no" will be defined as "maybe", "now" will be "later" and "stop" will be "continue".

- Telling a child, "You are a good friend"… Friend? Parents are not supposed to be friends with their children!

- Adding "Okay?" after assigning a child to do something puts the child in charge and the discipline in question. (What if the child says "No"?)

- When parents use questions to rebuke their children, such as. "When are you going to stop fighting?" or "Why haven't you cleaned your room?" they are not really soliciting answers. Disciplining children with questions sends a mixed message.

- Reprieve for good behavior, such as "if you stop crying you can come out" puts the child in charge.

Father Time is Always Near

- Respect for time measures a person's emotional health.

- The person who stays up half the night and then can't get up in the morning was overindulged as a child.

- The emotionally healthy person sets the alarm, gets up and never sets his watch ahead to fool himself into being on time.

Anxious Earlies and Lazy Lates

- A person who is always early is anxious.

- The person who is always late to appointments is essentially hostile.

- Mostly on time, rarely late and rarely early point to the well-adjusted person.

Ah, Mañana, Mañana

- People who behave as though life is forever will miss deadlines.

- Postponing a meeting when the agenda calls for ongoing discussion can throw progress into disarray.

Reliability is a Rare Virtue

- The instant person will tend to his responsibilities, respecting his own mortality. Life is a temporary condition.

- A person who says he will call at a certain time or pay a bill on a particular day and who does is reliable.

While the Fool Thinks it Over, the Wise Man Does Too

- When a fool, who in hope of winning an advantage, postpones an impending agreement, will often discover that the wise man has used this extra time to reconsider his own option and may leave the fool begging to reinstate the former agreement, but to no avail.

We're Entitled to Life, Liberty and the Pursuit of... Fun?

- People whose preoccupation in life is having fun, too often abuse alcohol, smoke cigarettes, overeat and use illicit drugs. Having been overindulged growing up, they want what they want when they want it, regardless of the consequences. They are remiss in not understanding that just being alive is fun and that in their pursuit of fun they cut their lives short.

- The emotionally healthy person sets the alarm and gets up on time.

- Postponing a meeting when the agenda calls for ongoing discussion, throws progress into disarray. Timing is "everything."

- The person who is always late to appointments is essentially hostile. A person who is always early is anxious. Mostly on time, rarely late and rarely early is a well-adjusted person.

Thoughts

- Inability to prioritize.

- Perfection is the enemy of good enough.

- No decision, is a decision.

- One's essence is as unique as a fingerprint and begins early in life intent on keeping the person alive. It is the person's psychological DNA which shows up in the person's every action as well as dreams

- A car repairman confronted a surgeon on whose car he was working and said 'we both repair bodies, only you get paid much more', to which the surgeon responded 'Try working on the car with the motor running'.

- Can you be too punctual?

- This country has to learn that as much as the intention of raising adored, worshipped children sounds good – It boomerangs!

- When a thing is damaged, it is not a catastrophe. When a person gets psychologically or physically damaged, it can be worrisome. One has to distinguish between the two.

- Less learning while growing up creates more mule-like work one will have to do in life.

- Old habits die hard.

- The automatic responses replace telling the truth.

- Mother's Day is a holiday for the insulted mother to savor every moment of neglect.

- One's eyesight deteriorates with age, so looking in the mirror at any age one still looks young.

- I regret that I regret.

- We must not walk around psychologically naked.

Old Habits Die Hard

- "I am smart enough to know what I don't know."

- "Worry itself doesn't change anything."

- "Don't pee on me and call it rain."

About the Author

Dr. Ruth Velikovsky Sharon learned at the desk of her distinguished father, Dr. Immanuel Velikovsky, a prominent psychiatrist and eminent man of science whose genius engaged even the mind of his friend and contemporary, Albert Einstein.

Dr. Sharon received a B.A and M.A. degrees from New York University and a Ph.D. from the Union Institute and University. She is a graduate of the Center for Modern Psychoanalytic Studies and a certified psychoanalyst.

Her books:

- I Refuse to Raise a Brat (co-author: Marilu Henner), 1999
- ABA - The Glory and the Torment, The Life of Dr. Immanuel Velikovsky, 1995, revised edition 2010
- Shame on You - You Were in My Dream, 2003
- Immanuel Velikovsky - The Truth Behind the Torment, 2003, revised edition 2010
- The More You Explain - The Less They Understand (co-author: John Cathro Seed, M.D.), 2005
- Imagine Art - Works of Art by Ruth Velikovsky Sharon, Ph.D. and Elisheve Velikovsky, 2009
- Art Catalogue, 2010

The More You Explain ...

The Less They Understand

by Ruth Velikovsky Sharon, Ph.D.
John Cathro Seed, M.D.

ISBN 978-1-906833-00-8

In this, perhaps the most encompassing of her works, Dr. Ruth Velikovsky Sharon brilliantly lifts the veil that shrouds the mystery of psychoanalysis, revealing intrinsic truths that can forever assist us in our journey to self-discovery and growth.

Harvard Medical School trained, Dr. John C. Seed's contribution of the Physical Health chapter will enlighten the medical community as well as the average reader, and if abided by, will help prolong life.

Shame on You –
You Were in My Dream

by Ruth Velikovsky Sharon, Ph.D.

ISBN 978-1-906833-01-5

Finally a new and easy guide to the understanding of dreams, which really makes sense! Ruth Velikovsky Sharon, PhD has developed a completely new understanding of the nature of dreams, which is fascinating because of its simplicity and its practical orientation.

In her book, Dr. Sharon describes the way that parents can be of help vis a vis dreams. She includes chapters on manipulation in dreams, dream catchers and other gadgets and the environment and dreams.

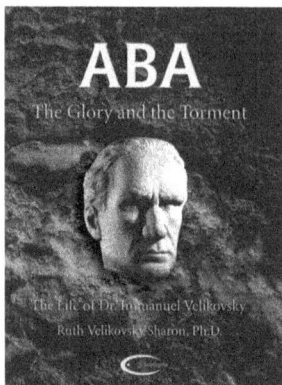

ABA – The Glory and the Torment

by Ruth Velikovsky Sharon, Ph.D.

ISBN 978-1-906833-20-6

In this book you get to know Immanuel Velikovsky as a person. His daughter Ruth describes his childhood, his family environment and his eventful life.

Using plenty of background information, numerous anecdotes and many photographs she makes us familiar with her father, but also shows the personal dimension of the devastating campaign he encountered to in the last decades of his life.

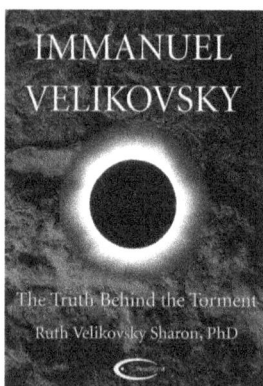

The Truth Behind the Torment

by Ruth Velikovsky Sharon, Ph.D.

ISBN 978-1-906833-21-3

In this supplement to her father's biography, Ruth Velikovsky Sharon, PhD. depicts the true facts about the campaign against him.

She publishes revealing letters in full length, that show the true nature of the undeserving - unscientific - treatment of Velikovsky by the scientific establishment, a treatment that appears rather medieval than enlightened.

Imagine Art

Works of Art by
Ruth Velikovsky Sharon, Ph.D.
and Elisheva Velikovsky

ISBN 978-1-906833-02-2

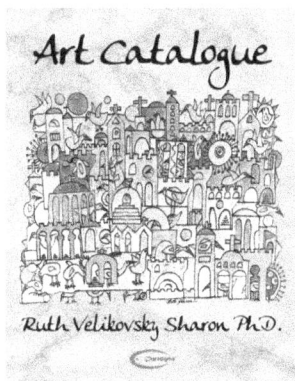

Art Catalogue

Ruth Velikovsky Sharon, Ph.D.

ISBN 978-1-906833-03-9

The name of Velikovsky is mainly known from the scientific and historical discoveries of Dr. Immanuel Velikovsky.

Far less known is the artistic dimension in the Velikovsky family, mainly expressed by Elisheva (or "Elis") Velikovsky and Ruth Velikovsky Sharon, PhD., the wife and daughter of Immanuel Velikovsky. For everyone interested in and fond of visual and plastic arts this booklet will give an exhaustive overview of the remarkable range of the works of these two artists.

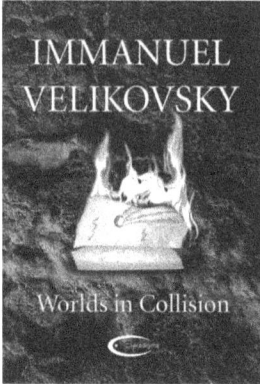

Worlds in Collision

by Immanuel Velikovsky

ISBN 978-1-906833-11-4

With this book Immanuel Velikovsky first presented the revolutionary results of his 10-year-long interdisciplinary research to the public - and caused an uproar that is still going on today.

Worlds in Collision - written in a brilliant, easily understandable and entertaining style and full to the brim with precise information - can be considered one of the most important and most challenging books in the history of science. Not without reason was this book found open on Einstein's desk after his death.

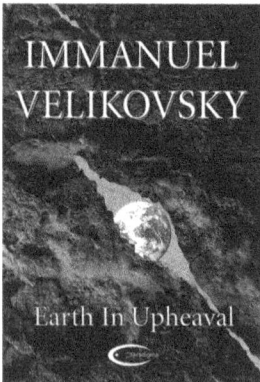

Earth in Upheaval

by Immanuel Velikovsky

ISBN 978-1-906833-12-1

After the publication of *Worlds in Collision* Immanuel Velikovsky was confronted with the argument that in the shape of the earth and in the flora and fauna there are no traces of the natural catastrophes he had described.

Therefore a few years later he published *Earth in Upheaval* which not only supports the historical documents by very impressive geological and paleontological material, but even arrives at the same conclusions just based on the testimony of stones and bones.

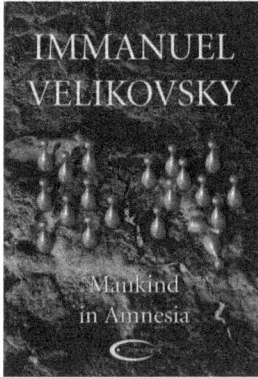

Mankind in Amnesia

by Immanuel Velikovsky

ISBN 978-1-906833-16-9

Immanuel Velikovsky called this book the "fulfillment of his oath of Hippocrates – to serve humanity." In this book he returns to his roots as a psychologist and psychoanalytical therapist, yet not with a single person as his patient but with humanity as a whole. After an extremely revealing overview of the foundations of the various psychoanalytical systems he takes the step into crowd psychology and reopens the case of *Worlds in Collision* from a totally different point of view: a psychoanalytical case study. This way he shows that the blatant reactions to his theories (which are still going on today) have not been surprising but actually inevitable from a psychological perspective.

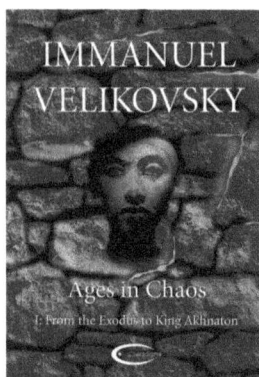

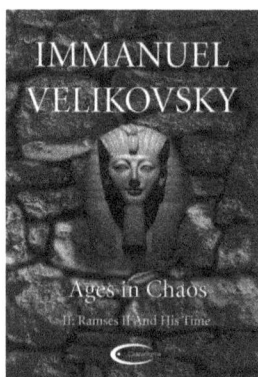

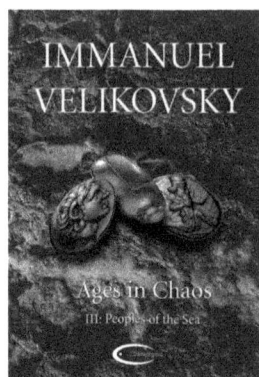

Ages in Chaos

Immanuel Velikovsky

I: From the Exodus to   II: Ramses II and His Time   III: Peoples of the Sea
King Akhnaton

ISBN 978-1-906833-13-8   ISBN 978-1-906833-14-5   ISBN 978-1-906833-15-2

In his series *Ages in Chaos*, Immanuel Velikovsky undertakes a reconstruction of the history of antiquity.

With utmost precision and the exciting style of presentation typical for him he shows beyond any doubt what nobody would consider possible: in the conventional history of Egypt – and therefore also of many neighboring cultures – a span of more than 600 years is described which has never happened! This assertion is as unbelievable and outrageous as the assertions in *Worlds in Collision* or *Earth in Upheaval*. But Velikovsky takes us on a detailed and highly interesting journey through the – corrected – history and makes us witness, how many question marks disappear, doubts vanish and corresponding facts from the entire Near East furnish a picture of overall conformity and correctness. In the end you not only wonder how conventional historiography has come into existence, but why it is still taught and published.

Just as Velikovsky became the father of "neo-catastrophism" by *Worlds in Collision*, he became the father of "new chronology" by *Ages in Chaos*.

www.ingramcontent.com/pod-product-compliance
Lightning Source LLC
Chambersburg PA
CBHW022125280326

41933CB00007B/547

9781906833046